Manchester Girl

Growing up in 1950s Manchester

Barbara Hull was born in Moss Side, inner city Manchester, attended Primary School in Chorlton-on-Medlock and spent her teenage years in the inner city. She worked and studied in the city until 1988. She now lives in North Yorkshire, UK

This book is dedicated to Bill Hull, my lifelong partner and the love of my life

Contents	Page
Chapter 1- The unique teenage experience in 1950s Manchester	4
Chapter 2 - What we ate	7
Chapter 3 - What we wore	16
Chapter 4 - Where we lived	25
Chapter 5 -The rich cultural mix	30
Chapter 6 -Education: some school-day memories	38
Chapter 7 - School-organised leisure activities	50
Chapter 8 - Gainful employment	53
Chapter 9 - Indoor Leisure Activities	57
Chapter 10 - Outdoor Leisure Activities	69
Chapter 11 - Relationships between the sexes	74
Chapter 12 – Holidays	82
Chapter 13 – Conclusion	85

Chapter 1 - The unique teenage experience in 1950s Manchester

The 1950s in the UK might be seen as a negative and bleak post-war period. Nothing was further from the truth. Manchester had and continues to have a unique vibrancy; growing up there in 1950s, we youngsters were imbued with a sense of civic pride: although you were not always sure how exactly life there differed from elsewhere, there was a real sense of being somewhere special. We were educated on the importance of the city and the significance of the Manchester Bee in the city's coat of arms, a powerful symbol of the city's strength. The industrious bee image is still a rallying symbol for Mancunians; witness its upsurge after the 2017 terrorist attacks on the city. Only later did I discover that indeed it was in Manchester that the first free library in the English speaking world, Chethams, had opened in 1653; that Ernest Rutherford, the father of nuclear physics had conducted his research; that Rolls and Royce had come together; and the Manchester Baby, the world's first electronic stored-program computer, had been conceived.

Living on Oxford Road in the city itself, which is relatively small, when compared to the *Greater Manchester* conurbation, meant that I was not far from anywhere of key civic importance – the central library, the cinemas and theatres, the University, the Manchester Museum.

At the time, only when I chatted with cousins from smaller Lancashire towns, like Preston, Nelson, Blackburn and Bolton, did I realise that my childhood experience in Manchester was very different from theirs and certainly more diverse and stimulating. Later on it was only when career commitments took me away from Manchester and I compared notes on childhood experiences with colleagues and friends, that I realised the extent of my good fortune at being born a Mancunian! I left the city over 35 years ago, but when I am asked, in conversation, where I am from, I still reply, "I live in Yorkshire now, but I'm really from Manchester."
Manchester was the big city, cosmopolitan compared to smaller Lancashire towns of the time. This enriched everyday life in the city. It had the largest Jewish community outside London; over the years there had been incoming waves of Irish immigrants seeking work; its university welcomed academics and students from all over the world. This cultural diversity gave, and still gives, Manchester a unique piquancy. It was "multi-cultural" before the term had been coined.

This book's broad coverage is life for a 1950s teenager, considering the various elements of school and work and the available opportunities for relaxation and entertainment. It is written from two perspectives, the first based on the actual memories of someone living their teenage years in the inner city, the second reflecting on subsequent changes to everyday living. So, each chapter recounts some aspect of life in the city at that time, followed by a reflection putting the lived experience into its wider context.

I must stress that this is a very *personal* account based on my own life experiences and may not assign great attention to some aspects that others may find more significant.

Chapter 2 - What we ate

Not much of a choice of things to eat in 1950s Britain! Although war rationing was largely over, the range of available foods was extremely narrow, compared to today. Till the mid-fifties much of our food was seasonal; entry into the European Union and easy foreign travel had not yet whetted the appetite for such exotica as garlic, olives, pâté, wine and vegetable oils. It was common knowledge that across the Channel they consumed frogs and snails on a daily basis and us Brits knew better than eat such "foreign muck". It would be many years before garlic, capsicums and courgettes would become widely accepted, or even available, in this inner city territory. The choice of ingredients and their relative scarcity meant that we ate "good plain food" – this usually meant a fairly small serving of meat and two veg. one of which was always potatoes; we also ate a lot of cabbage, swede and carrots. Cauliflower was considered a bit "posh" and usually reserved for Sunday when you had the big meal of the week, dinner (eaten at midday). This meal was often graced with a pudding, usually milky rice or semolina or apple pie. Tinned fruit and salmon with salad were treats reserved for Sunday tea and, if it was a special occasion, we might even have cake and jelly and custard!

Most households made a traditional effort to have a piece of meat to roast for Sunday dinner but it had to last till midweek. It was eaten hot, in a rationed amount, for Sunday dinner, then maybe some cold at Sunday teatime. After that the bone was scraped clean and the bits would appear variously recycled in "Resurrection Stew" – scraps of meat boiled up with onion, carrot and potatoes; "Meat balls" – scraps of the meat mixed with breadcrumbs, formed into little cakes and fried in lard. The bone was boiled up with pulses to make a weekday broth. A corny old joke tells of a vicar's wife asking him to say grace before their meal but he refused saying that this wasn't necessary as the meat on the table had been blessed at least three times already.

Sunday was the day when, if it was getting "serious", you invited your boyfriend or girlfriend to Sunday tea, to meet your family - quite a nail-biting occasion for all concerned.

Hollywood films with scenes in restaurants serving a wide of exciting foods used to set me dreaming and wondering if WE would ever enjoy that kind of luxury. I wanted to move on from painful penance to pagan pleasure! Not that here was anything wrong with the meals my Mum prepared, apart from their lack of variety. They were delicious and I am grateful to this day for the basic, but important, culinary skills she taught me: how to make a good soup out of practically nothing and the art of producing light pastry. I do remember eating a lot of stewing beef, shin beef and shoulder steak, but we also ate every part of the beast: oxtail, cowheel, tripe, lambs and bull's hearts, sheep's head, liver, kidneys, lights, fries (testicles) In skilled hands, and with long slow cooking, they could be transformed into delicious meals. Buying meat was also a skilled activity to source good ingredients.

When I asked my mother why the butcher left the rabbit's head on the skinned body when that part was not eaten she explained that this proved it was not a cat! Apparently when skinned, it is difficult to tell them apart. All these unusual cuts of meat are no longer easily available as the pre-packaged meats in supermarkets have largely replaced the traditional butchers' shops and I do miss them for the variety of possibilities they offer for inventive cooking. I believe they now find their way into factory-prepared dishes. Young people often express horror when I tell them of the parts of the animal we used to eat then but in all probability they too are still eating them, but unrecognisably processed into their frozen burgers and pizzas.

Our monotonous diet would have made Elizabeth David despair but it had been born of the rigours of rationing. When everyone was talking about the end of rationing and saying we would be able to buy as much as we wanted, my reaction was that, although it was a mite repetitive, we had enough already.

As a young child I had been told about the joys of the pre-war era when you could easily buy bananas and nuts. I couldn't wait. What a letdown! My very first taste of banana had been a real anti-climax, although nuts were a different-matter. Other fruits such home grown apples, rhubarb, pears and plums, had been available but in limited quantities and I promised myself that, when things improved, as I was sure they would, fruit would become my indulgence. I fantasised about not being reprimanded for being greedy with the fruit bowl. Ken Dodd was right when he said, "They're dead posh, they buy grapes when nobody's ill". Noteworthy that there were very few obese children in those days, in fact very few obese anybody.

But eating in Manchester did offer some definite opportunities for sampling the exotic: there was quite a rash of curry restaurants around the Oxford Road, University area, serving mainly chicken curry and rice at knock-down prices, possibly reflecting a foreign student demand. These restaurants would ultimately be transformed into what the Guide books now call the "Curry Mile". The presence of this "otherness" did impact on my tastes. At home from a very early age I had been fed a pseudo curry, made with curry powder, my mother's aim being "to get you used to eating different things". My small town cousins were appalled.

For anyone in search of true exotica, the first Chinese restaurant in Manchester city centre, the Ping Hong, had opened in 1948, offering a hugely exciting experience to make forays into unknown territory.

"Did you know they eat *fried* rice?!"

"No!! Rice is for making rice pudding"

The owners of the Ping Hong had astutely devised an ordering by number system. All the dishes on the menu had a Chinese name with a description in English and a number, so you were spared the embarrassment mispronouncing in Chinese. The subsequent growth in Chinese restaurants in Manchester would lead to a corresponding growth in the services developed to serve them and their customers. This would become more pronounced when the city centre area became the focus for the Chinese community in the whole of the north of England on Sundays - the day most Chinese in takeaways and restaurants take off. Then the area really comes alive as the community comes into the city centre to promenade and chat, visit Chinese medicine shops and health centres, visit Chinese financial and legal services, pop in and out of the shops and supermarkets and drop the children in at the Sunday schools. In this way Manchester Chinatown has become the Chinese village for the north of England.

There had always been an Italian presence, largely of ice-cream makers, in Manchester; they lent a wonderful feeling of excitement and colour to the legendary Manchester Whit walks where, unlike other contingents, they carried their magnificent colourful statues. The 1950s witnessed a general developing interest in things Italian, fashion and food and especially Italian coffee bars, mainly in the city centre; I remember particularly El Vino's on Oxford Street where I tasted my first cappucchino ever and felt very sophisticated. The pop song, "Volare" won Italy third place in the 1958 Eurovision Song Contest; nobody could understand a word of it but it sounded so romantic that my friend and I learned it phonetically so that we could sing it at parties to impress everyone! There is a Manchester Italian Association flourishing to this day (and they *still* parade their beautiful statues at Whitsuntide!)

1953 saw the end of wartime sweet rationing. For years we had made a weekly trip to the sweetshop to buy our 2 ounce allocation of sweets. These years of deprivation had clearly had an impact on the collective British psyche and the heady experience of being restricted only by the size of your wallet was too tempting for most. A vivid memory is of visiting the sweetshop on the very first day of non-rationing and being confronted with shelves full of row after row of empty glass jars.

The de-rationing of sweets had a dramatic effect on the confectionery market. I have since read that spending on sweets and chocolate jumped by about £100m in the first year to £250m - a year which, according to the confectionery industry, was "as dynamic as any in the industry's history". It seems that UK consumers now spend in excess of £5.5bn on confectionery each year.

Our only real takeaway was the "chippie", the fish and chip shop which sold fish, chips and mushy peas, sometimes meat pies and suet puddings. They were cheap so there must have been a ready supply of fish.

However, it was fairly unusual for people to eat outside the home. Housewives making regular calls on the chippie's services for family meals were considered lazy and inadequate. The chippie was a treat if you on a day trip. Other possibilities on days out in Lancashire were cheap plates of respectable tater hash served on marble-topped tables at Yates's Wine Lodge. Sadly it was seen as a bit down market and my mother threatened me with dire consequences if I ever told anyone where we had had lunch at Blackpool. Yates's is still in existence today, but gentrified beyond recognition.

On days out with my father we invariably had lunch at the imaginatively named UCP (United Cattle Products) which specialised in offal. Their speciality was a legendary tripe and onion dish. I still love tripe, now really hard to find in the UK. Strange how other nationalities were less keen to abandon offal. When Sophia Loren visited Manchester for a book signing in 1979 and stayed at the Midland Hotel, everyone was curious about her diet and the Manchester Evening News sleuth reported that for dinner she had eaten *Fegato alla Veneziana* - liver and onions to you!
Whenever I'm on holiday in Europe, I take the opportunity to eat offal, still revered and prepared with respect and love.

Chapter 3 - What we wore

Clothing rationing had only just ended in 1949 and old habits don't fade overnight. Clothes were still precious and recycling or wearing of "hand me downs" did not have any stigma whatsoever. An item of outgrown children's clothing, "with some wear still in it" would be passed around families and friends. Today one hesitates to offer unwanted clothing in this way for fear of giving offence and the Charity Shops have now assumed the role of recycling still usable items.

The rag and bone man was still a common sight. For a bag of unwanted items he rewarded you with a "donkey stone". These scouring stones, used for cleaning doorsteps and named after their trademark donkey imprint, were made from powdered stone quarried in Wigan and Northampton. Many working class women, as a matter of pride, washed and donkey stoned their front door steps daily.

The rags were sold on and I have seen them recycled quite imaginatively - the least worn part of men's trouser legs could become a pencil skirt, the best bits of a woman's dress could be cut down to make one for a little girl.

A favourite re-use for really worn heavier fabrics was to cut them into strips and, using a special pegging tool, fix them to a piece of hessian, to make a fireside rug. Depending on what was available, making a rag rug in this way could offer great scope for creativity. Surprisingly, nowadays you can still find instructions of how to make a rag rug on Youtube.

More immediate access to discarded clothes was via "Big Annie", a redoubtable Amazonian lady who had a twice-weekly stall on Denmark Road Market, Moss Side. The real attraction was her delivery: she had a huge bag of second hand clothes and presented them to the crowd as if they were haute couture. The price would start quite reasonably, say 7s6d (37.5p) but no-one bought anything at the first price as they knew this was a Dutch auction and it would fall steadily with Annie sounding more and more irritated at the lack of response until finally she would bellow, "Eighteen pence" (7.5p) and the item would be rolled up and hurled at the final taker.

 I never bought anything but it was cheap entertainment with a lot of good-natured banter. Annie must have made a decent living or she would not have kept running the stall, which she did for years.

As the decade progressed, for new clothes there were various possibilities: Manchester had once been dubbed Cottonopolis because of its central role in the Lancashire cotton industry and there were numerous outlets for fabric, especially cotton, by the yard; department stores, specialist fabric shops and market stalls offered a grand array of fabrics for the home dressmaker. A huge favourite for a staggering range was Bachers Fabrics in High Street; sadly, reflecting the then decline in home sewing, it would go into liquidation in 2003.

All girls did basic cookery and needlecraft at school, even in the academic Grammar School. We were gravely informed when we were deemed to have gained sufficient sewing skills to "make a garment". This took the form of a cap sleeved cotton dress with a frilled yoke, the pattern being supplied by the school with a choice of cotton fabrics from the supply in the Sewing Cupboard. The resulting garment, whilst not exactly cat walk, was indeed wearable and I even spotted some of these very distinctive "school made" dresses when I started work in an office.

Having been taught needlecraft in school, many women could sew a simple garment and, failing that, there was a ready supply of seamstresses to create something unique. Manchester and indeed all of Lancashire had a long relationship with textile production. Both of my parents, like so many others, hailed from mill towns and had started work in the cotton mills at age twelve. At school we were told that because of its damp climate, Lancashire was perfect for spinning and weaving as the thread was less likely to break. By the eighteenth century Lancashire was the biggest producer of textiles *in the world* and every Manchester schoolchild could tell you about James Hargreaves' invention, the spinning jenny. Everyone knew the old adage, "Britain's bread hangs by Lancashire's thread"

Knitting garments was also normal behaviour for *girls*; the few boys who found it interesting, did so in secret! There was a definite gender bias of approved activities. You learnt to knit either from your mother or grandmother but also at school. It was quite common for old outgrown hand-knitted sweaters to be unravelled so that the wool could be used again.

There was something quite satisfying about knitting, the rhythm of the needles clicking having a very calming soothing effect. However, its thrifty homespun image meant it was to fall seriously out of favour as prosperity increased but it would enjoy a remarkable resurgence in the 2010s when it became "cool" to knit.

Another common occupation for women in this era of make do and mend was darning. Many socks were made of wool which tended to wear holes at the toe and heel. "You've got a tater in your sock!" was a common expression. Provided the hole wasn't enormous, it could be quite satisfying to make it disappear using a "darning egg" which looked like a wooden or Bakelite mushroom, to provide a smooth surface inside the sock and a darning needle and matching wool to weave a small patch to cover the offending hole. The activity was really seen as female, hence the humour and pathos in **the Beatles**' 1966 song "**Eleanor Rigby**", when McCartney sings about the priest Father McKenzie: "Look at him working, darning his socks/ In the night when there's nobody there." Again I was amazed to find Youtube videos demonstrating the art of darning.

But, like everyone else, I hankered after something new and frivolous. Hollywood films provided us with plenty of ideas for the unattainable. As a young teenager, I dreamt of having a wardrobe full of bright, colourful, new clothes that had not had any previous owner and the possibility of wearing a different outfit every day. De rigueur would be a long, very full, red skirt, preferably circular. These desires were typical of the time and 1950s fashion was dominated by voluminous skirts underpinned with lacy underskirts sometimes with a hoop through the hemline to make it stand out. The other thing I hankered after was pretty underwear and diaphanous nighties! Because of the lack of central heating most nightwear had tended towards flannelette. Really beautiful underwear would only make an appearance in the 1960s. Nevertheless changes were on the way and less sensible attire was becoming available. The real biggie for reasonably priced ready-made clothing for men, women and children was C&A Modes (popularly known as "Coats and Ats") on Oldham Street. Sadly, the firm stopped trading in the UK in 2000, although it is still thriving in the rest of Europe.

In the 1950s it was where you went to get reasonably priced clothes with various nuances of quality. The prices always ended with 11 pence. The very cheapest dresses were nineteen shillings and eleven pence, 19/11d (just under £1) and the quality rose through 29/11d, 39/11d to the utter decadence of 99/11d (just under £5 which doesn't seem much, but this was an average week's wage). The sales were even more fun. As late as the mid-70s, a very chic French friend of mine, on a visit from Paris, was thrilled to find a dress for just £1 in the Manchester C&A sale.

There were of cause smaller clothing outlets which, although they did not give credit, offered the possibility of "laying aside" an item. The item was put away in a drawer in the shop and the purchaser paid however much they could afford each week until the full price had been paid when they could take away the item. The credit card and its accompanying problems was not yet with us. If you did not have the ready money, you did not have the goods!

There were also catalogue clubs the main one being Littlewoods. Again they offered no credit. The members clubbed together and week by week, when there was enough money in the kitty, sent for each member's choice from the glossy pages.

An easy way to get a "new look" was by dyeing old clothes a different colour and it usually worked very well as most clothes were made of natural fabrics which would take the dye. Trying to dye manmade was usually disappointing; the dye just seemed to stay on the surface of the material. Dyeing could be professionally done but it was great fun to buy a dye for a shilling at the corner shop and do it yourself. Recently thinking of revisiting this activity from the past, I was very disappointed by the limited range of dyes available in local shops; it is clearly no longer a mainstream activity, but who knows what austerity will bring? I did find what I wanted on Amazon!

Shoes were not very exciting and had to last. There were "cobblers" everywhere to replace both soles and heels and the shoes were never as comfortable once the soles had been replaced. You could also do shoe repairs at home with stick on soles and heels; an internet search indicates that they seem to be making a comeback, another instance of the present decline of the throw-away society?

The profligacy displayed by the emerging Teddy Boy cult was a sharp exception to the general feeling of 1950s thriftiness. Their clothes were an adaptation of Edwardian style and featured long, sometimes past the knees, tailored jackets with velvet collars and drainpipe jeans or trousers, skinny ties, and chunky crepe-soled leather shoes, popularly known as "brothel creepers". The look was completed with long hair combed into what looked like the back of a duck called a D.A. or Duck's A,,, Teddy boys can be seen as a key element in the development of the youth cult in the UK.

Chapter 4 - Where we lived

In the early part of the decade, really just post-war, there still remained many bombsites around the city, although the later 1950s witnessed a building boom. What is now deemed standard for a private dwelling, e.g. central heating, was seen as highly luxurious then and new homes were still being built without it. Many lived in old houses without bathrooms, and running *hot* water was a rarity. The use of deodorants was just beginning. Consequently, keeping properly clean was not easy and it was fairly normal for many not be as "fresh" as we are today. It is to the credit of Manchester City Council that they provided reasonably priced wash baths and laundry facilities at the city's swimming pools, although some preferred the legendary tin bath in front of the fire. It was fairly standard practice to have a bath and wash one's hair only once a week, usually Friday night; the occasion was made more special by the addition of perfumed Imperial Leather "bath cubes", manufactured by Cussons of Salford. Some of these 1950s bath cubes, still in original packing, were recently for sale on ebay – the force of nostalgia! It is good to read that Cussons is still flourishing around the world.

All teenage girls crave a bit of glamour and we were no exception. This could often be achieved through using perfume (or "scent" as everyone called it then). The great favourites were Californian Poppy, Phul Nana and Bourjois' Evening in Paris (dubbed locally by detractors as "Midnight in Moss-Side"), all relatively cheap at the chemist; I remember buying Phul Nana for my mother's birthday for about two shillings (10p). Nostalgia took me to internet searching which revealed that Californian Poppy is no longer made but has a near substitute, Bourjois stopped making Evening Paris in 1969 but my Mum's favourite, Phul Nana, is now a luxury item at £210 a bottle!

White goods were pretty rare: practically no-one had any kind of washing machine or refrigerator and televisions were very rare; the occasion of the Coronation in 1952 was a great spur for television sales but they were still out of the financial reach of many, but for this special event many of the better off invited less affluent friends to their houses to watch the event.

For many of us keeping clothes clean was a rather tortuous process with a number of possibilities: washing by hand which could be extremely arduous, depending on how dirty the clothes were; there was a copper boiler which ran on a coal fire or gas but was not suitable for everything, really just for cotton.

Drying could be quite a problem in rainy Manchester. Many houses had a ceiling rack for wet clothes which could not be dried outside. There were also free standing "maidens" which went in front of the open fire. So, if Monday, the traditional washing day was wet, the kitchen was full of steam! Things could take a long time to dry and in the meantime could be well impregnated with whatever was being cooked in the kitchen. No wonder people looked elsewhere to keeping clothes clean.

The City Council provided Wash Houses where you could do your laundry; just appearing were Laundromats. It was fairly common to use laundries, often Chinese, which had the reputation of being very thorough. The main problem with laundries was the laundry mark, used to aid identification of items' owners. It consisted of a strip of tape with a brief ID in indelible ink, which was attached to each item. It seemed quite ridiculous when attached to a handkerchief. However if you paid extra and elected to have a "bag wash", your laundry was washed separately from everyone else's and the ID strip was not necessary.

Central heating in private houses was practically unknown and most homes had a coal fire with a black lead grate, often incorporating an oven and sometimes a back boiler to heat water. Fireplaces made of ceramic tiles were objects of desire, status symbols out of the reach of most ordinary folk.

Bedrooms were not heated unless someone was seriously ill. In winter you could see your breath on the bedroom air and the windows were often covered in ice on the *inside*. It was normal to get undressed for bed in front of the fire downstairs and then dash up to bed as quickly as possible, clutching a hot water bottle. In the depths of winter people often put their overcoat on top of the insufficient blankets on the bed, but it was still possible to spend a full night in bed without ever getting warm. When duvets started to make an appearance in the late 1950s they were like manna from heaven.

Some houses still only had an outside toilet, so during the night any calls of nature had to be satisfied by a 'pot de chambre'. What joy when you finally moved to a house with an inside toilet! For many, as a result of the post-war slum clearance policy, this would be a council house.

 Huge overspill estates were built outside the inner city areas in places like Langley and Wythenshawe. The houses were of a high standard of construction with inside toilets, bathrooms and gardens front and back. Friends who moved there loved the houses but missed the animation and familiarity of the inner city. In the rush to rehouse a maximum number of people as quickly as possible, the planners forgot that people need more than a place to live. Initially the estates had no cinemas, pubs or shops and people had to return to the city centre to satisfy these needs.

At one stage in my teenage years my parents took over a rather woe-begotten old pub in the city centre and I never lived anywhere else till I married in 1961. I always enjoyed all the advantages of city centre life but I did envy the comfort of those modern houses on the new estates...

Chapter 5 - The rich cultural mix

Diversity was an everyday reality. Unlike my cousins in smaller Lancashire towns, I grew up in a multi-cultural, multi-racial community. There were many elements in the Manchester melting pot.

When post-war reconstruction and construction of the motorway network started, there were succeeding waves of Irish immigration, mainly from Eire, and consequently Manchester had a higher than average number of Catholics. At that time my parents had been live-in caretakers at a University building and from the age of 4 I had lived on Oxford Road not far from the Roman Catholic Church of the Holy Name and have an indelible memory of droves of Irishmen coming out of the church after the 11 o'clock Mass on Sunday, spruced for the occasion and wearing their Sunday best. This was remarkable because there were so many *men,* as most had left their families in Ireland and sent money home weekly. Also, while they were very well turned out for church, their best suits were very different from English tastes as they had a penchant for what seemed to me a very bright blue! For an Anglican, it was strange to see such a horde of people at a church on an ordinary Sunday!

Once a friend persuaded me to attend Mass, which at that time was still in Latin. I had studied Latin at school and so could understand most of what was being said. My friend was very amused when I expressed amazement that all these labourers were proficient in Latin, which is far from easy. She showed me the Missal with the Latin on the left and the English translation on the right. "We don't understand it word for word. Just recognise the opening sentences so we know where we're up to!"

I thought the Irishmen had a strange way of speaking. Apart from their impenetrable accent, they addressed all men as "Mister" and women as "Lady".

A lot of them lived in boarding houses in the working class area of Chorlton-on-Medlock, near the University. My friend's Mum ran one of these boarding houses, which she ruled with a rod of iron. As her paying guests worked hard at manual jobs, she fed them what seemed to me to be gargantuan portions of bacon, potatoes and cabbage. I sometimes pitched in to help my friend Veronica whose job it was to peel enough potatoes for eight hungry navvies. Mrs O'Leary bought them by the sack! I sometimes joined them at table and have never lost my taste for the humble boiled spud, the thing I miss most if I stay away from the UK for too long.

As a teenager I was once invited to an Irish Club in Collyhurst. I found it pretty much like any other drinking club but was amazed when at closing time everyone stood up and acknowledged their Irish roots by heartily singing "The Minstrel Boy"

When I had my first job in the Tax Office I met many of these Irish construction workers who visited the office to sort out their tax problems. Initially I was quite shocked to discover how many were illiterate and signed their names with an "X" and how many did not have birth certificates for their children, just certificates of baptism. There was great rivalry between Catholics and Protestants as to who had the best processions during the legendary Manchester Whit walks week, a 200 year- old tradition: Protestants walked on Whit Monday, Catholics in Whit Friday but most Mancunians enjoyed watching *both* processions: there was a definite touch of the carnival to proceedings. My father, a Baptist by religion, often sang the praises of the "Hidden Gem" the Roman Catholic church in Mulberry Street, central Manchester. This was a typical attitude, pride everything that Manchester had to offer.

The most colourful and exotic Whit procession was the separate Italian one organised by the Italian immigrant community. Instigated in 1890 it still takes place today in full vigour whereas the others have been moved to Whit Sunday and are less well supported and ostentatious than previously. The Jewish population gave the city an extra dimension. They lived largely in the Cheetham Hill area, at walking distance from the railway station that had disgorged the original arrivals, fleeing pogroms across Europe and carrying all their worldly goods. They represented a kind of "otherness" , sometimes hard to understand e.g. the strict dietary laws and observance of the Sabbath by refraining from any work, which included lighting a fire and cooking a meal, but they had coping strategies for this! A delicious slow cooking stew, Cholent, was put on a low light on Friday and 12 hours later eaten for lunch on the Sabbath. In these pre-central heating days a fire could be lit on the Sabbath by a non-Jewish person, a "shabbos goy" – an easy way for gentile kids to earn a bit of pocket money if they lived close by.

Many Jews were active in the rag trade and there were any number of skilled Jewish tailors and dressmakers in the Cheetham Hill area. Doing business with them was an interesting experience, giving me my first encounter of haggling over prices, an activity they really seemed to expect, enjoy and recognise as part of the process. Often when I bought an item of clothing from a Jewish shop, I left with the invocation, "May you wear it in health" which I haven't heard for years. Jewish dressmakers would provide me with a unique wedding dress and trousseau when I married in 1961. Many Jews were sincerely grateful to have been received as refugees in the UK. One of them was our cobbler, who regularly expressed his gratitude to God for the English Channel, for separating us from Europe, saying "That water is worth £5 for every egg cupful". The Jews offered a great object lesson in survival and would leave a mark on the city's public and commercial life.

I also met non-Jewish survivors of the concentration camps, Latvians, who had been allowed to settle here after the war. Many had been wealthy in Latvia before the war so in the camps their experience had been made less harsh by being able to buy a few privileges, like fresh vegetables. When they arrived in the UK they had to take menial jobs in the NHS but they generally adapted well. As members of the privileged classes, they had been well educated and many spoke English, German and French. I loved to hear accounts of their pre-war life and was impressed by how well they adjusted to the changes thrust upon them. We kept in touch with one such couple for a long time after the 1950s. Our children used to refer to them as "Uncle Ziggie" and "Auntie Val"

Since the end of the war there had been a Polish community in Manchester. As now, they had the reputation of industriousness and had their own clubs and social welfare network. I remember being invited to and receiving a warm welcome at the Club Polski in Cheetham Hill.

The 1950s also saw the arrival of the Windrush generation in the UK and whilst most seemed to aim for jobs in the capital, a good number of Jamaicans settled in Manchester with many finding jobs in the NHS, public transport and engineering factories. Their colourful clothes, music and exotic tastes were another dimensional spice added to the overall mix.

There were also a large number of Nigerians, both workers and students. The existence of the University of Manchester and UMIST was a magnet for scholars from all over the UK and the world and again this added depth to everyday life.

The 1950s also saw the arrival of the Sikhs in Manchester – yet another element in the mix! We learnt about the importance of the wearing a turban for men and, when quite a number found jobs as bus conductors and drivers, where regulations stated that wearing a peak cap with identity number was obligatory, there appeared to be an impasse as they refused to remove their turbans. Good old British compromise won the day and it was not unusual to get on a bus staffed by Sikhs with the identity badge attached to the turbans! The city took them to its heart; they were applauded in Albert Square by the general populace for their help to victims after the terrorist bomb attack in 2017, when they had opened their temples to offer food and shelter to those effected.

There were also Indians who had mostly come work in the textile mills and other factories. They brought with them their memorable cuisine which proved popular with the locals; chicken (or beef) curry and rice would become a frequent focus of a night out and we soon learned the nuances of heat between Korma, Madras and Vindaloo! Later on their string of restaurants on Wilmslow Road, Rusholme would become known as the Curry Mile.

I am grateful for the opportunity of meeting so many nationalities at an early age. No, it was *not* an idyllic society with no racial or religious tensions. Newcomers did experience name-calling and cold shoulders from some but there was little physical violence. Negativity was often reprimanded by others. I remember once at school an African man coming to complain that one of the pupils had been calling him "Blackie" in the street. The culprit was identified and apologised and for a while afterwards we ragged her "Did you see any *green* men today? - Have you seen any *purple* men recently? - I haven't seen any *orange* men, have you Pat?"

Chapter 6 - Education: some schoolday memories

Every day began with Assembly, a corporate Christian act of worship, which is apparently still a legal requirement for non-faith state schools. We used to line up outside the Hall. It was quite a formal procedure; we lined up in year order and marched in to our allotted spaces to a piano accompaniment. At Grammar school there was a handful of Jewish girls who waited outside till the religious element was over and were then called in for the day's notices. I enjoyed assemblies because I liked singing the hymns and there was always a teacher who could play the accompaniment well. We had a Religious Education lesson once a week and I must admit that, as no exam was involved, most of us saw it as a chance to relax for 45 minutes.

Christmas was always celebrated with a Carols Concert and a Nativity play. There was keen competition to be the Virgin Mary and sometimes lots had to be drawn to ensure fair play.

Although a corporate act of worship is still a legal requirement today, a 2017 survey found that a quarter of secondary schools break the law by failing to conduct one. One of the results of today's multiculturalism is that many children are not as familiar with the central tenets of Christianity, a pity as our language and literature are full of biblical references – "judas sheep", "scapegoat", "casting pearls before swine"- to name a few.

Corporal punishment still operated in schools – leather strap on the hand – the humiliation of being punished was worse than the physical pain but most teachers did not use it. There was no need; roles of teacher and pupil were clear and respect was shown by addressing male teachers as "Sir" and female teachers as "Miss". In the poorer inner city, those children who had problems in keeping clean at home were encouraged to come to school early to get washed; it was low key, matter of fact. Some teachers even made toast for disadvantaged children before school started.

Another over-riding school memory is of the regular visits of the "nit nurse" who inspected everyone for the presence of head lice which were rife in poorer areas. The infested child was given a letter to take home and advice on how to clear the infestation which was no respecter of the degree of cleanliness of the hair. Nevertheless, a huge sense of shame was attached to being given a letter by the "nit nurse" and, if nothing was done at home to remedy the situation, the infested child would have to have their head shaved, the ultimate indignity, especially for a girl. Imagine that I today's PC world! I was lucky in that, although I did qualify for a "nit nurse" letter once or twice, I never had my head shaved. The horror of shaved heads was probably subconsciously linked in the collective psyche to the images of female collaborators being punished at the end of the war. Strangely enough, I cannot remember the shaved children ever being subjected to any name-calling from the rest of us; we all just felt really sorry for them, saying not to worry, it would soon grow back. I believe the problem of head lice is still in our schools but no doubt is dealt with in a less draconian way.

School milk was free, as were dinners for the poorer families. Dinners were paid for in cash at the beginning of each week and tickets issued to each child, blue for payers and white for freebies. It was not unknown for free tickets to change hands for half the normal price between "poor" kids and "rich" kids. Then with these liquid assets both could enjoy a change from school dinners at the local chippie. Generally speaking though, we enjoyed our school dinners; the picky eaters of today had not yet been born, there were no vegetarians, vegans, allergy sufferers. It was meat and two veg (always potatoes but *never* chips and a preponderance of cabbage, mushy peas, carrots and swede). Older Mancunians will remember the puddings with great affection – syrup suet pudding, tapioca or semolina milk pudding but for me the star was the Manchester tart, a traditional English baked **tart** consisting of a **short crust pastry** shell, spread with raspberry **jam**, covered with a **custard** filling and topped with flakes of **coconut** and a **Maraschino cherry**. Apparently it remained a staple on Manchester **school dinner** menus until the mid-1980s. School dinners were available in the school holidays at "dinner centres" and for many children this was their only proper meal of the day. Sadly, newspaper reports tell us that the situation is again current. During the Covid 19 crisis the famous Manchester United footballer, Marcus Rashford, would speak up, and, citing his own experience, stress the importance of the free meals in the school holidays. His action was later recognised by the award of an MBE.

The general atmosphere in schools was so different from today, far more frugal. Ball point pens were just making a general appearance but were banned by many teachers, the rationale being that they made writing easier and not everyone could afford one. The school provided "dip in" pens and ink and it was deemed quite an honour to be ink monitor trusted to fill up the inkwells. An increasing number of pupils did have fountain pens and these would gradually be superseded by ball point pens.

There was of course no Information technology. Even the humble calculator had not yet made an appearance. We had to have enough knowledge of arithmetic both to keep track of our own money and for the world of work. We learnt times tables (up to 12X12) by heart and I can still remember them today. Some offices and workshops did have small printed "Ready Reckoners" to help with calculating money transactions. In pre-decimal currency days, before 1971, it could be quite time-consuming to calculate, e.g. the cost of 17 items at £2/4/11½ each, when the 2 represented pounds, the 4, shillings (with 20 to the pound) and the 11½, pence (with 12 to the shilling). I believe the "Ready Reckoner" concept still exists, for calculating specific sums such as winnings on horse races, redundancy payments and roof building.

Some of the textbooks we used still bore the logo "this book conforms to war economy standards". All textbooks issued had to be returned at the end of the year and whilst in use backed in brown paper, or even newspaper by the recipient, to make them last longer.

Paper was precious. You were handed a single sheet of paper to complete your homework assignment.

I was fortunate enough to enjoy the benefits of a grammar school education; comprehensive schooling had not yet been introduced and we were sifted into types at the age of eleven, those with academic potential, those showing technical leanings and the remaining "hewers of wood and drawers of water". The Eleven Plus exam had a paper of "Intelligence tests" and for some children the first time they encountered them was on the day of the exam. It is often said that with this kind of test, practice improves performance and children in wealthier areas were coached in their idiosyncrasies. As an inner city child I was very fortunate in having Mr. Chester, a progressive teacher who tried to redress the balance by giving us intelligence test training too. In the event the challenge provided by the tests was great fun and I continued to enjoy them even after the 11+ exam! The exam had to be taken anonymously at a central location and we were issued with identity numbers which we were terrified of forgetting; I remember mine to this day, G1038. Our teacher explained gravely that the girls had been given numbers prefixed G and the boys prefixed B so that the examiners would know our gender and ensure that an equal number of boys and girls would pass. We saw this as reasonable thing, not realising that it represented a shifting of the goalposts to make the number of successful candidates fit into the places available in the existing single sex schools. Today it would certainly raise feminist hackles.

The 11+ exam has been much maligned but it did give some bright working class children wider horizons and greater opportunities. Unlike many other inner city pupils, a number of us from my school (about 30%) did pass the Eleven Plus and I became a pupil at one of the most prestigious girls' grammar schools in the city. What a shock to the system! I was rubbing shoulders with girls whose parents were university professors, doctors, company directors. In my junior school most of my friends' dads were either manual workers, unemployed or just non-existent. I learnt then that the junior schools in affluent areas, had had an almost 100% pass rate in the Eleven Plus.

Grammar school was all a pretty scary new world. Perhaps the worst part was the extra-curricular activities. A large proportion of my new classmates took elocution lessons and played musical instruments. Girls passing LAMDA exams were feted at morning assembly when they were summoned to the platform to receive their certificates. I had to ask what LAMDA was (London Academy of Music and Dramatic Art, apparently). Could I survive in this alien world? The Eleven Plus was hailed as a fair instrument to facilitate social progression; hence the anonymity of the written exam. I have to say that I did benefit enormously on an academic plain. I still appreciate the opportunity of learning Latin and French, the first steps in what would be my lifelong love affair with languages. There was a handful of girls from the wrong side of the tracks; we conspicuously caught the bus home to the city centre on the opposite side of the road from everyone else.

In the early weeks I fretted that all these self-confident middle class companions were far more intelligent than me but I need not have worried. By the end of the first year I had gained the reputation of being the class brainbox and won the class prize for "General Proficiency". At the annual Speech Day it was now my turn to go on the platform to receive my prize! Speech days were an important occasion at the Manchester Free Trade Hall with prizes and certificates presented by Kathleen Ollerenshaw, later to become a Dame, an amazing woman, who was known nationally for educational reform and lived all her life in Manchester, serving on the Education Committee. She would become Lord Mayor in the 1970s. Many years later I would read her full biography and was duly impressed by the personal obstacles she had overcome and that she had taken time out of her high-flying career to attend a girls' school speech day.

Reflecting on the differences in wealth at my school makes me appreciate, with hindsight, the discipline of school uniform. It had given me first-hand experience that it is really is a great leveller. My Dad, a pub landlord, was reasonably well off and had made sure that I was fully kitted out on the uniform front. He was haunted by early memories of working class kids of his own generation who had passed the exam for grammar school but had had to decline because the family could not afford the uniform. Besides strict conformity to uniform rules were particular rules on hair: the back of the neck had to be visible, which meant either a very short haircut or pigtails. Make-up and jewellery were not permitted and this policy was .vigorously applied. I remember an incident concerning a friend of mine, who was stunningly beautiful naturally, with peaches and cream complexion, long black eyelashes and blonde hair. She was admonished for wearing makeup and sent to wash it off. When she insisted that she was not wearing any makeup the teacher concerned backed down but did not apologise. I loved wearing earrings and in order to be able to wear pierced earrings out of school, I had to arrange to have my ears pierced on the first day of the 6 week summer holidays so as to have the necessary 6 weeks for them to heal with the gold sleepers in place, without healing over.

An interesting side issue was that my new classmates, when they found out where I lived, realised that I had more colourful experiences to share with them, especially when it emerged that I lived in a pub, and, from age 13, sometimes worked (illegally) behind the bar! I must admit that I made things sound rather more racy than they really were, just to see their dropped jaws. Manchester education policy insisted on weekly swimming lessons for all children and the vast majority did learn to swim and pass the test of swimming for 25 yards. The Victoria Baths, Hathersage Road, now a listed building and museum, was at that time, still in use for these lessons. Children walked around a mile to and from swimming lessons. Unlike today, there was very little childhood obesity!

Chapter 7 - School-organised leisure activities

Many teachers organised out of school activities, sport, drama, field trips but I remember especially with great pleasure the English Country Dancing twice a week after school. We even made it to the Manchester Schools' Country Dancing Festival where we did not win any prizes but were highly commended. Thank you. Miss Hennessy for your time and enthusiasm. It left me with an enduring love of folk dance and music.

In the 1950s "ordinary" people did not go on foreign holidays and few held a passport. I felt very privileged to go on a school-organised trip to Venice at aged 15. We travelled on a collective passport, all the way by train, taking about a day and a half! When we changed trains in Switzerland for Italy, we were shocked to find that the seats were bare, un-upholstered wood.

The trip was an experience that changed my life, providing a dramatic contrast to the bleak colourless world of northern England. We stayed in a convent and we all appreciated the authentic pasta dishes we were served, nothing like the tinned spaghetti we were used to.

One day, as a special treat the nuns served a very strong tasting vegetable that no-one would eat. It was chicory and no-one had ever eaten it before. The nuns were very crestfallen and after being reprimanded by our teacher we all dutifully ate a small portion each.

This trip made us realise there are other ways of living and for me was the beginning of my lifelong fascination with la Bella Italia. It was also my first experience of foreign boys, quite different from Brits. All this would not have been possible without our languages teacher whose organisational skills had made it possible at an affordable price. Thank you Miss Foley, I am grateful to this day. The Halle orchestra was based in the city providing a huge bonus that we did not appreciate at the time. Sir John Barbirolli ran an outreach programme for Manchester Schools – special concerts, designed to appeal to children and young people, especially those who might not be exposed to classical music at home. While it was smart to pretend to one's peers not to enjoy them, seeds were definitely sown! Only years later, did one realise fully the privilege of attending these live concerts performed by an orchestra of international reputation, and I bought a season ticket for the Sunday Halle concerts.

Compare today: schools can download from the BBC website 10 pieces designed to appeal to children. This is very convenient but, like so many other modern experiences, lacks the real experience of going to a concert have someone playing just for *this* audience.

My grammar school drama group also staged plays, almost at professional standard. This is where I saw *The Admirable Crichton* and the *Importance of being Ernest* for the first time. Apart the entertainment value, such projects built self-confidence imbuing us with a "can do" approach to pursuing our goals. One or two girls from these productions even went on to act professionally. On one occasion we even put on a Jean Anouilh play, *Antigone*, a Greek tragedy written in French. For various reasons – my French was good and I was tall enough to play a man and I looked OK in my Dad's trousers – I was persuaded to play Hemon, Antigone's lover. It went fairly well, as it was only a small part, but I realised, there and then, I had no future aspirations to Thespianism.

We generally worked hard in school and as a reward one afternoon a week we had a "hobbies" session when teachers shared their enthusiasm for their own hobbies with the girls. It was quite an eye opener to see their other side such as the amazing sight of our very strict Latin teacher demonstrating the finer parts of Swedish weaving. You could join a different group each term with the aim discouraging us from becoming too swotty and focussed on academic matters.

Chapter 8 - Gainful employment

In the 50s there was no problem for school leavers in getting a job. Although it might not be the job of your dreams, it never occurred to you that just getting any job would be a problem. Anyone leaving school in 1950s with GCE 'O' levels, had a huge choice of job opportunities in the many city centre offices. Lots of clerical staff were needed in pre-computer days! It was a centre of banking, insurance, accountancy and many of the mail order catalogues had their offices there. After leaving school in 1957, I started work as Tax Officer with H.M. Inspector of Taxes. At my interview I was proudly informed that the five day week and equal pay had just been introduced. This concept was still causing some debate generally: everybody knew that "a man should be paid more because he has a family to provide for "and women only work "for pin money".

Working a full day was a real shock to the system, after the relatively short days I had experienced at school; I thought the day would never end. Then there was the office politics to become familiar with but you soon became part of a "community" which did things together, like an annual day trip to the seaside and Christmas party in the office. For me, the product of a single sex school, there was the added complication of working with the opposite sex. In an office of over 50 staff there was always a bit of flirtation in the air. Although I did not, many of my colleagues would meet their life partners at work; apparently it is still the second most popular way to meet your significant other.

Less academic school leavers also found ready employment, as Britain was still a manufacturing nation and post-war rebuilding and reconstruction was ongoing.

There were also ample opportunities to learn a trade as an apprentice which usually took 6 years and often included a day a week at College to study for the related City and Guilds examination. Apprentices were often general dogs' bodies and received a tiny wage, but it did lead to a recognised qualification. New apprentices were traditionally the butt of practical jokes such as being sent to another department or even a neighbouring business to ask for a bucket of steam, a left-handed screw driver or a long weight. This was part of their initiation into the world of work and was fairly harmless. A friend of mine was sent for a long weight and disappeared for the rest of the day, only returning just before home time. "Where've you been?" his supervisor demanded. "I went for a long wait, like you said." After that he was not sent on any more wild goose chases.

As a Tax Officer, I had to deal with many tax problems and, for the fair number of the Irish immigrants who were illiterate, had to complete their tax forms and witness their X's. Many of my colleagues could not understand their strong Irish accents at all but I acquired an ear for them and was often called on to "interpret". (I would later go on to become a French and Italian translator/interpreter so maybe I got some useful training there!)

Many years later, when university degrees became less rare, a friend of mine with a good Honours degree was recruited as a Tax Officer, to do the same job I had landed with 5 GCE 'O' levels in the 1950s.

At the same time as working in an office, I also worked as a barmaid several nights a week saving all my wages and tips for package holidays. A school trip to Italy had whetted my appetite for foreign travel and there was a huge post-war boom for all inclusive trips to southern Europe. I went on a coach all the way to San Sebastian in Spain and had my first taste of sunburn and Spanish tummy to prove it! After seeing "Three coins in a fountain" and "Roman holiday" I went to Rome, threw my coin in the Trevi fountain and have been back numerous times since.

Chapter 9 - Indoor Leisure Activities

Museums and Galleries

For an inner city child, the Manchester Museum was a favourite haunt – free access to a mind-boggling collection. Firstly it was very close to where I lived, secondly I was impressed by the sheer size of the place with a whale's skeleton suspended from the soaring ceiling, thirdly there was the Egyptian mummy, which I proudly took out-of-towner family members to see. It was much later that I became aware of the international status of the Manchester Egyptology collection. It must have made a powerful impression on me; in later years it would become a favourite wet Saturdays outing with my own children! My youngest son, who still lives in Manchester, is also keeping up the family tradition with his children.

The same thing applied to the Manchester Art Gallery, again free and within easy access. I still visit whenever I am in Manchester, so gaining a double pleasure, seeing the art work and reliving my childhood.

This where I fell in love with, among other exhibits, the Pre-Raphaelite paintings. At the time I did not know they were famous, I just instinctively responded to them. Only later did I discover that this is one of the most revered collections in the country and had a secret smile when a Yorkshire friend excitedly told me about her Art Club trip to Manchester to see the Pre-Raphaelite collection. She was rather surprised that I knew several of them by name, e.g. the Light of the World, the Hireling Shepherd, even though I had not been on the trip!

When I think about it, I gained a great deal from the ready access at an early age, to these facilities. The experience certainly sowed seeds, making me more receptive to art and appreciative of other collections elsewhere. I did not set out with any high flown ambitions of self-improvement. It was just somewhere to go, that did not cost anything and often just to escape the Manchester rain. I have since heard what happened to me is called "education by stealth"

Sometimes when public funds are tight there is a temptation to see Museums and Art Galleries as non-essential frills when in fact they answer a very basic, if not immediately apparent, need. Just think of those cave dwellers thousands of years ago. They had no electricity, no computers, no mobile phones, but they found the time, energy and materials to paint their walls with most amazing art work, some of which is still visible today.

Reading and Libraries

In the early 50s most people did not have access to a TV although a great boost to sales of TVs was the televising of the Coronation in 1952. By the end of the fifties over three quarters of the population had access to a television set. It was a massive change: people discussed what was on TV, cinema audiences dwindled and television became a part of nearly everyone's life. But change was gradual and at the start of the 50s reading and libraries were a cornerstone of entertainment. Manchester has a long history of commitment to library provision: **Chetham's Library** in the city, which claims to be the oldest public library in the English-speaking world, opened there in 1653.

As a teenager I was an avid reader and using Manchester Public Libraries in the 1950s, my expectations of library services were high. It came as quite a shock when I moved to live in another authority area, that not every council gave libraries the same emphasis. Manchester was generous with its eligibility for library membership: anyone living or *working* in the city could join. This meant that people who commuted from surrounding areas and boasted of paying minimal local rates had the same access as those living in the city which rankled those paying the higher rates needed to provide proper services.

Manchester had been the first local authority to provide a public lending and reference library after the passing of the **Public Libraries Act 1850**. The Manchester Central Library, in its "wedding cake" circular building, inspired by the Pantheon in Rome, opened in 1934, was the cathedral of the public library service and there were numerous branch libraries throughout the city. The prominence of the service was a source of civic pride, trumpeted in schools and we were all encouraged to make full use of its facilities. The basement of the Central Library housed The Library Theatre Company, whose home it would be for 58 years. It began in 1952, with a production of Oscar Wilde's hilarious comedy, *The Importance of Being Earnest*. Over the years it would offer opportunities to such future icons as Janet Suzman and Alan Rickman. Because of its bijou size, it provided a wonderfully intimate bond between the actors and audience. It must have been heavily subsidised because it was very affordable.

With all these first-class facilities available I found it strange that people also *paid* to borrow from private libraries such as Boots and numerous corner shops, which provided copies of popular fiction. Sometimes it is assumed that if you have paid for something, it must be better. Additionally, there were some local authority librarians who saw their choice of books as an opportunity to educate rather than entertain and refused to stock popular fiction.

By the end of the 1950s interest in reading was waning because of the "easy fix" of television.

Cinemas

Till the 1950s the cinema had been king. There were cinemas all over the city, some more prepossessing than the others referred to as "bug huts". On Oxford Street In the city centre there was a whole string of cinemas: the Gaumont, the Odeon, the Regal, the Oxford. Going to the cinema was often the venue for a first date and any cinema visit, especially city centre, counted as "going out" and worth getting dressed up for. Local cinemas were very familiar places, certainly not luxurious but neither was the price. As a child and teenager I went to the cinema regularly, three times a week. In local cinemas, the same film was shown Monday, Tuesday and Wednesday and then a different one for Thursday, Friday and Saturday and changed again for Sunday.

There were also cinema clubs for juniors on a Saturday morning, with entry costing 6 old pence. Films produced in the States were generally considered superior to British offerings; they provided a glimpse of unheard luxury and we were probably subliminally persuaded that everyone in the States was financially better off than we were.

The 1950s saw a BIBLICAL-EPIC FILM craze, *The Robe, Quo Vadis, The Ten Commandments, Ben Hur, Solomon and Sheba, David and Bathsheba*, to name a few and I saw them all! I still enjoy my very grainy copy of *The Robe* from time to time. Could be Richard Burton...

There was strong competition for courting couples to get seats on the back row, which afforded them a kind of privacy they could not easily find elsewhere. The American equivalence would be in a car, but these were not very common here in the 1950s.

The centrality of the cinema in our lives is evidenced by the popularity of British-produced fan magazines, *Picturegoer* and *Picture Show* which only ceased publication in 1960 with the corresponding children's comic, *Film Fun,* lasting until 1962. Nevertheless, the fifties were a decade of change; black and white televisions were appearing in the homes of the better off. Watching television was more of a social activity than now. The "haves" often invited the "have-nots" to watch specific programmes. Video recorders would not become readily available until the 1970s so people would often rush home to see a favourite programme or refuse other social invitations rather than miss the final episode of something.

It is interesting that even though nowadays cinema attendance is severely reduced, the big screen is still offers an experience that cannot be easily replicated with home entertainment, notwithstanding the interruptions of those who forget to turn off their mobile phones.

Theatres and Music halls

Aplenty! Manchester received many stars of international fame, such as Nat King Cole and Billy Eckstine. The Palace Theatre even hosted a Royal Command Performance in 1959. King's Hall, Belle Vue also saw artists of international fame, including Louis Armstrong in 1959

Recorded Music

The younger generation was beginning to call its own tune, showing its own musical preferences. We were assaulted by the vocals of Johnnie Ray, most famously singing "Cry" with real tears. Then Bill Hayley and the Comets burst on the scene with the film "Rock around the clock" which had everyone dancing in the cinema aisles with the really wild element using the occasion as an excuse to vandalise seats. It played to packed houses all over Britain, with some local authorities banning it from being shown. In Manchester I went to see it at the Gaiety Cinema, Peter Street. The council allowed it to be shown but banned it on Sundays!

But all this was before the advent for the "King", Elvis Presley, whose first single "Heartbreak Hotel" was issued in 1956, having a very disturbing effect on many teenagers, including me! It was the first gramophone record (78 rpm) I ever bought. Henceforth, I bought every single one on the day they were issued, even before I had heard them. Elvis was a very real part of my adolescence and I've since met hundreds of women who felt the same way. It would always be a disappointment that the "King" never visited the UK, but we did have our home-grown pop singers, like Cliff Richard, Tommy Steel, Terry Dene.

On a more sober note, the Playhouse Theatre, Hulme housed a repertory company with a different play each week and tickets were affordable. Plays were also performed in smaller venues such as the Green Room and the Library Theatre.

Pubs

The pub was high on the list of leisure activities. There were "Town pubs" where you went smartly dressed with someone you wanted to impress, or who wanted to impress you. I remember being taken to Frascati's on Oxford Street and feeling as though I had "arrived", due partly to the name of the venue. City centre pubs had started to serve cocktails, aping the exciting drinks you had seen in Hollywood films.

It was also possible to drink at the bar in the Midland Hotel's Wyvern Room. The Midland was the hotel in Manchester where visiting celebrities stayed so it felt special to go and have a drink there; who knows who you might bump into? It's where I took my Forces pen pal there in 1959 when he finally came home from Aden and we met face-to-face for the first time. Like many teenage girls at the time, I had started our correspondence after I read an appeal in the newspapers.

Unlike town pubs, the local pub really was the social centre for the immediate area and everyone knew everyone else and all their business. Coronation Street was most definitely drawn from life. My Dad was landlord of a local pub so I had first-hand knowledge. Board games were popular: cards, dominoes, cribbage and darts. Gambling was illegal but there was frequently money on the table! Off course betting on horses would remain illegal until 1961 but again nearly everyone did it and any local pub worth its salt had a bookie's runner. I sampled the joys of a flutter at a very early age but soon gave it up when I did the sums and realised that the bookie always wins.

Darts were popular, played on a Manchester or "log end" dart board, reputed to offer a more challenging game than a standard one. I believe the boards are still made today. Our pub had both a men's team and ladies team. We belonged to a Darts League, "St Mary's Darts and Social Club" my father's brainchild. Match nights were fun, made special with sandwiches (and pickles) at half time and a raffle. How much excitement could you take? The real gala occasion was the final of the darts league; this warranted a Lancashire hotpot supper. To cook for so many required organisational skills of military calibre. I do remember having segs on my hands after all that potato peeling. The hot pot was cooked for three hours in a slow oven in two enamel buckets. Because an ordinary domestic oven could only take one bucket at a time, the other one was farmed out to a neighbour on the promise of a few free pints. The proper accompaniment was mushy peas which again took some organising, given the quantity required. They were soaked overnight in a baby bath and cooked in the four largest pans we could get our hands on. In this pre-throwaway society we also had to borrow plates and cutlery. This somehow made the event more special because everyone felt involved.

Our pub, in an area of two-up two-down terraced houses really was the social centre, a refuge from bleak homes, some still lit by gas. In winter the customers appreciated the physical warmth of the pub as much as anything; we always had two open coal fires and after my Dad persuaded the brewery to install central heating, the regulars packed in like sardines; when "Time gentlemen please" was called, no-one wanted to leave.

Like lots of pubs in working-class areas, or pub was only licensed to sell beer and wines (which at the time meant port and sherry). After a long day's manual work beer was just what the customer wanted and it was relatively cheap: mild beer cost one shilling a pint (5p) and a pint of bitter one shilling and two pence (6p). I always found it rather sad that a lot of men, with their wages in cash, would call in on a Friday night, for a quick pint on their way home and end up staying till closing time, going home with a sadly depleted pay packet. My father, ever practical, consoled me with the observation "If they didn't spend it here, they'd spend it somewhere else". I have since learned that it really is a bad idea to advise anyone on how to spend their hard earned money.

On a Saturday night the wives would appear and the men would abandon their usual haunt, the "vault" or "tap room" to sit with their better halves in "the room" as the lounge was called. This was the era when Babycham (termed Champagne Perry at the time) was making an appearance. As the landlord's daughter, I was often treated to a Babycham, which cost slightly more than a pint of bitter; its main attraction was the glass it was served in a Champagne coupe emblazoned with a coloured Bambi, making you feel just like a film star! I believe that Babycham is still available today, but following a court case, can no longer claim to be Champagne. Personally, nowadays, I prefer a nice dry Prosecco!

Chapter 10 - Outdoor Leisure Activities

Parks and open spaces

Local parks were well frequented. They were of key importance at weekends and during school holidays as few people had a car to drive into the country. A favourite plant in all the parks was the Rhododendron, which must have been suited to the acid Manchester soil. I loved their large exotic blooms. Given the persistent rain in Manchester, covered shelters, always referred to as "the shed", were provided in parks. The parks were supervised by a kind of security guard who gave chase if you were seen interfering with the plants and kept an eye out for loutish behaviour. The nearest to the city centre, Whitworth Park, although small, also housed the Museum of Textiles. The parks did have their fair share of strange men and I was quite stressed out when I saw my first "flasher" in Whitworth Park.

A much larger park, Platt Fields, a little further out of town to the south, had a popular boating lake and a number of other features but my favourite was the Shakespearian Garden which was said to contain all the plants mentioned by the bard. Platt Fields continues to be valued with Friends of Platt Fields Action Group committed to preserving it.

Heaton Park to the north of the city is even larger. It was destined to receive the Pope on his visit to the UK in 1982

Although the 1950s was the period when car ownership expanded dramatically, at the beginning of the decade, car ownership was fairly rare amongst the general population. Some of those without cars satisfied their need for green spaces in the city by catching the bus to visit the huge, 76 hectare, Southern Cemetery where John Rylands (of John Rylands Library fame) was buried. It was a haven, albeit rather sombre, for inner city dwellers. Wandering among the graves on a hot summer's afternoon certainly led to reflections on the transience of life. The cemetery opened on 9 October 1879 and had mortuary chapels for **Anglicans, Nonconformists,** and **Roman Catholics** linked by an elliptical drive and a Jewish chapel at the west corner of the site. The original cemetery is now registered by **English Heritage** in the **Register of Historic Parks and Gardens** for its historic interest and the mortuary chapels and other structures are **listed buildings**.

The cemetery was destined to receive the mortal remains of many famous Mancunians, such as Sir Matt Busby and the founder of Factory Records, Tony Wilson. Though it does not have the same kudos of *international* spread of the defunct, a visit there is somewhat reminiscent of the Pere Lachaise cemetery in Paris.

A Manchester friend told me that is was a convenient retreat to meet a friend there for a chat during the Covid 19 social distancing period. We Mancunians are very resilient!

Sport

As a teenage girl, I was fairly disinterested in sport myself but I was aware that there were many opportunities in the city to practice and spectate sport: football, athletics, cricket, swimming, running. Fans of Manchester's two football teams demanded that you supported one or the other! Sometimes people said that United was largely Catholic and City Protestant but to me that was irrelevant, as, like many girls at the time, I was not being particularly interested in football anyway. Nevertheless, like everyone I did feel a certain pride in both teams as they formed part of the Mancunian identity. I will always remember the shock and horror of hearing about the Munich air disaster in 1958 when the airliner carrying players and backroom staff of Manchester United, crashed in a blizzard on its third attempt at take-off. Twenty-three of the forty-four passengers on board the aircraft lost their lives and all Manchester mourned them.

Other spectator sports interests were available at the Belle Vue complex which offered greyhound racing in the country's first purpose-built stadium: racing as well as boxing, wrestling and speedway. It all served to give the city that extra buzz that made you proud to be associated with it, even tenuously.

My Dad used to go to watch the cricket at Old Trafford if the weather was good and would fall asleep in the sun; it must have been exciting to watch!

I knew that Manchester Harriers, founded in 1886, was active in the 1950s and is still going strong today.

Sport was practised and encouraged in schools and if, like me, you had two left feet and couldn't hit a ball straight, it was a bit of a nightmare. During tennis lessons my similarly sport-phobic friend and I used to hit the ball over the fence and spend the rest of the lesson "looking" for it. I would learn many years later that I did have an undiagnosed co-ordination problem but times were different then: I was just seen as clumsy. One sport I did enjoy was swimming which was prioritised by the City Council. In my school it was the proud boast that *everyone* had passed the length (25 yards) certificate. Could have also been the influence of the Esther Williams films which were hugely popular with their performances of synchronised swimming.

What was noticeable was the class divide on practising sport after leaving school. Many of the middle class continued to play sport but apart from a kick-about with a football in the street, the working class tended to leave playing sport behind once they left school. By contrast spectating, especially football, was largely a working class pastime.

Scouts and Guides

Like many other 1950s teenagers, I was an enthusiastic member of a guide group for a while. We seemed to welcome the order and regimentation and sense of belonging and having the chance to do things we couldn't do at home, like sleeping under canvas and lighting cooking fires just with wood. Most scouts and guides were affiliated to a church; ours was run by the Rector's wife from Christ Church, Moss Side. I have wonderful memories of a week's camping in the countryside with lots of outdoor fun. On the Sunday the Rector visited us and set up an open air altar in the field for our Sunday Communion service, a powerful image I will never forget. We had all promised as part of the Guide promise "To do my duty to God and the Queen". Times change and I am told by a current Guider that this is no longer part of the promise. Apparently it was good for us as I read recently, "Analysis of a study of 10,000 people found ex-members [of scouts and guides] were 15% less likely than other adults to suffer anxiety or mood disorders at the age of 50", and we thought we were just having a good time…

Chapter 11 - Relationships between the sexes

In the 1950s most secondary schools were single sex and I went to an all-girls' Grammar School. There were pluses and minuses to this segregation; it eliminated one source of distraction during lessons, hopefully allowing more concentration on the lesson with a possible improvement in subsequent exam achievement. The strange unintended effect it had in my school was that any male of any age or appearance - window cleaner, postman, painter - who had the temerity to set foot on the school premises became the object of our nascent adolescent lust and likely to be consumed under our predatory gaze. St. Trinian's had nothing on us!

A really negative consequence of never having spent any normal activity time learning to work in a mixed sex group meant a steep learning curve when you were thrust into the world of employment, where you were expected to act normally in the presence of some gorgeous example of masculinity. You also had to learn to deal with what would now be called sexual harassment, mostly "double entendre" remarks. This was a no-win situation as, if you admitted to understanding them, you were deemed to be "a bit fast" so the easiest way to kill the sport was feigned innocence and incomprehension. No fun if there is no reaction!

In the event many lifelong relationships did begin in the workplace, which at that time had much more of a permanent community feel, in contrast with today's zero hours' contracts, hot-desking ambience and working online from home. Perhaps one of the less-acknowledged aspects of being unemployed is the feeling of not really "belonging" anywhere.

Of course teenage girls could and did also meet boys outside of work; there milk bars, pubs, friends' houses, church groups but the most popular place was at a dance. There were dances organised by various groups and organisations; I remember going to Boots (the Chemists) Staff Dance, because my friend's aunt worked there. In Manchester, as in other cities, there were commercial Palais de Danse and in this Mecca dancing led the way. These dance halls were a much safer haven for young teenage girls compared with today's clubs. They were there for *dancing* – no alcohol was served on the premises, just coffee and soft drinks. Some patrons obtained a "passout" which involved having a rubber stamp on the back of the hand, going to a nearby pub for a quick drink and on return proving one's right to re-admission by showing the rubber stamp.

Two girls would often dance together until they were split up by a pair of boys. This meant that the boys did not have to suffer the ignominy of being refused when they plucked up the courage of asking someone to dance. If you were "split up" in this way, good manners dictated that you did dance that one dance with the boys who would sense whether it as worth asking you again later. If you were not actually dancing, a boy would ask "You dancing?" The smart reply was "You asking?" – "I'm asking" - "I'm dancing". If things were going well on the dance floor, the boy would ask to "see you home" especially if you were from the same part of the city.

When this happened you usually made a date to meet again, often to go to the cinema. The sequence was almost ritualistic.

There were different types of dancing, the more athletic "jiving" type which had developed as an offshoot of the "jitterbug" we had seen on American films. Girls were generally better at this and it was not unusual to see the boy almost standing still while the girl danced round him, just grabbing his hands as a steadying influence. There were also the three traditional dances quickstep, foxtrot and waltz where the couple danced in unison, with varying degrees of competence. It was fairly rare for the band to play a tango, which gave the "proper" dancers a chance to show off a bit. The most popular was the last dance which was always, by tradition, a waltz.

Dancehalls were where many people would meet their life partners, whom they were more likely to marry than just cohabit with, a behaviour largely reserved for film stars. The swinging 60s hadn't yet arrived!

The Ritz ballroom Manchester had its own band, led by Phil Moss, as I recall, and was the place to be seen on a Saturday night. There was a rotating glitter ball in the middle of the ceiling which cast shooting stars on the floor when the lights were dimmed. How relatively easy it was to convert large room into fairyland by dimming the lights and installing a glitter ball, its magical spots of light creating a chaotic pattern over everyone's clothes, which always seemed more luxurious in this enchanted atmosphere. The real highlight of the evening was when the dancers were cascaded with hundreds of coloured balloons, just like New Year's Eve.

We were probably a lot less demanding and sophisticated and more easily satisfied than today's teenagers. Entrance to the Ritz on a Saturday was the most expensive in the week, five shilling (25p). I'll never forget that fateful evening in 1959, when looking my best in a homemade dress with a very full skirt and multiple starched underskirts a la 1950s, I saw a handsome bronzed god approaching me to ask for a dance.

Recently returned from two years' national service in Malaya, this Adonis swept me off my feet and less than two years later we were married. Like me, most of my friends met their future husbands at the Ritz. It's still there, was designated a Grade II **listed building** in 1994 and is now a live music venue and it most certainly sells alcohol!

The other Mecca dancehall in city centre was the Plaza, which saw the beginnings of the disco era with a DJ by the name of Jimmy Saville who ran Saturday afternoon and weekday lunch hour discos where entry cost 3 old pence (just more than 1p). I always found him a bit irritating, very egotistical and more interested in talking about himself than playing the records; we'd have much rather spend the time listening to such favourites as Elvis Presley belting out *Jailhouse Rock* or Frankie Lymon protesting that he was *Not a juvenile delinquent.* My irritation at Saville's ego would become something far stronger when the full truth of his activities emerged after his death.

There was also almost free entrance for females to the dances organised at Universities' Student's Unions, to compensate for a serious misbalance between the sexes in the then student population. This was an easy way to meet people from other backgrounds.

The Roller Skating Rink at Birch Park was also a good place to meet the opposite sex in a relaxed atmosphere but not as easy as going dancing; you had to learn to skate and either own a pair of skates or take a chance on those available for hire. The Rink would later become the Oceans 11 club for popular music acts.

The easiest place to meet anyone in the warm weather was in the park, or even on a bus or in the street but many considered this not quite proper. "Picking someone up in the street" just was not done. My mother firmly warned against associating with "street corner lads", deemed to be an unknown quantity of undesirable provenance. What would she have made of online dating?

Whilst most of us were trying to meet the opposite sex, we were not unaware of those "on the other bus" as my father used to describe it, or "batting for the other team". From an early age I had been aware that there were boys who preferred boys and girls who preferred girls and found this unfathomable but do not remember any nasty comments or violence against them, rather sheer incomprehension and a fair amount of leg-pulling and good-natured ragging. Manchester city centre was then, as it still is today, a haven where everyone could be themselves. The area around Canal Street was a well-known haunt and on a current Manchester tourist street map is clearly labelled "Gay Village"

I am remembering the times well before the 1967 Act which would legalise sexual acts in private between men. At the time I did know of some men who had married women for the sake of appearances, to deflect suspicion thus avoiding the threat of blackmail and extortion.

When I was a teenager my father took over a city centre pub, on Higher Cambridge Street, and doing a stint as a barmaid was a very educational experience. As a thoughtful teenager, I realised that a lot of the customers in the pub seemed to be "slumming it". Why else would someone who worked as an international representative for a major chemical company, or a BBC musician, be drinking in such a downmarket pub in the roughest part of Manchester? Easy! Because no-one questioned your sexual proclivities and you were accepted just as you were.

I was also not unaware of money transactions for sex taking place, but this did not prevent me from sharing polite small talk with "les girls" who were, for the most part, rather pleasant, if not very bright, young women. I also had a number of friendly acquaintanceships with gay men who, to my delight, enjoyed discussing girly things like earrings and makeup.

A very moving memory from that time is of Mary, one of "les girls", having a short visit from her teenage daughter, who had been taken into care some years previously. She asked me to spend some time with her daughter, explaining the girl had no idea of her mother's lifestyle and pleaded for my discretion. I was happy to oblige. As Mary also helped out as an occasional waitress in the pub, we were able to give the impression that this was her main source of income. Touchingly, Mary's regular clients also all played along for the duration of the daughter's brief visit.

This was an era of great life lessons for me. Yes, I learnt English, Maths, Science, History, Latin and French at Grammar School but I learnt human tolerance in the rough and ready inner city.

Against the recommendations of my headmistress, who wanted me to stay at school to study A Levels, I could not wait to leave school and left at sixteen. By eighteen I had met the love of my life and was married at twenty.

Chapter 12 – Holidays

Foreign travel was practically unknown for most ordinary people in the 1950s. Some people went to stay with relatives in another part of the country and that counted as going "on holiday". Blackpool (on the Fylde coast) was a one-week destination for the holidays of many in the northwest and offered a whole gamut of accommodation from quite prestigious hotels on the front to rather rough-and-ready boarding houses, ruled with a rod of iron by landladies, graduates of the GENGHIS KHAN SCHOOL OF CHARM. The rules were draconian: although contrary to Ken Dodd, there was *not* an extra weekly charge for the use of the cruet, there were other rules: you did have to stay out of the building all day, even if it was raining, and, in this pre ensuite era, access to bathroom facilities was limited with an extra charge if you actually wanted to take a bath. The profit margins must have been small because they were affordable, and, up to a point, this made the rules acceptable. Back home you could always give the impression that you had stayed somewhere more luxurious. As a younger teenager I stayed in such an establishment with my mother and sister, as my father had to stay at home to work. This was pre mass-banking ATM days and so the money for the week had to be taken in cash, which was hidden in a specially constructed pocket inside my mother's corsets. I have since seen variations on this theme – secret pockets sewn into the inside of trousers, bras, shoes.

A major pastime was walking along the promenade where there were freelance photographers snapping the crowds every few yards. The prints would be ready for collection later that day and many were bought as holiday souvenirs; I still have some of them, in my photograph collection. In the 1950s ownership of cameras was not universal and consequently photographs had much more of a rarity value.

Vivid memories of Blackpool in the 50s include the huge queues for the public toilets, which we seemed to accept as normal, our expectations must have been much lower then. Pleasanter memories included the excitement of riding in a horse-drawn landau, making you like a film star, something to drop into the conversation back home. The trams, running along the prom also figured prominently in the experience as Manchester had stopped using them at the end of the 1940s

For those who could not even afford a boarding house experience, day trips on a coach or "chara" were popular; there were also regular departures from Lower Mosley street coach station to escape from the city for the day. Ownership of private cars was fairly uncommon. I read recently that in the early 50s only 30% of travel was by car whereas today it represents the majority.

Holiday camps, Butlins and Pontins, were growing in popularity but, as I remember it, were seen by many younger people to be rather pricey. My Dad paid for the whole family to go to the Butlin's Mosney camp, in Eire which he deemed to be good value as all the meals and activities were included. It was fun with lots of organised activities but, although I didn't tell him at the time, it did remind me the regimentation of school with e.g. "first sitting" and "second sitting" for meals. I think we were more "obedient" then. I believe this Mosney camp has now become a facility for asylum seekers.

Manchester city council, like other local authorities. recognised the need for holidays and paid to send poorer Mancunian children on holiday to Ormerod House in Blackpool. I never went, as I had holidays arranged by my parents, but friends who did gave positive reports. I believe it still exists today to provide a respite at the coast for the less fortunate of the North West.

Chapter 13 - Conclusion

The recorded **history of Manchester** began with the **Roman fort** of **Mancunium** in A D 79. Manchester, the cradle of the industrial revolution, "Madchester" the home of great popular music, was, according to the Telegraph, ranked no.3 in 2013 UK tourist destinations because. "There's always something going on in Manchester, whether an international festival, a Premiership football match or a high-profile musician performing in one of the city's many venues. The buzz of the place is contagious, and new bars and restaurants are opening every week, serving everything from cicchetti to sushi."

Maybe it's something in the air but Manchester has an unsquashable character. It could be that horrible drizzly rain that builds up defiant resistance. "What doesn't kill me makes me stronger".

It has been the target for a number of terrorist attacks. A huge the IRA bomb wiped out the centre of the city in 1996 but people just said "They might have taken our heart but they will never take our soul". More recently the Manchester Arena bomb killed 22 and injured over 50 and reaction to this again demonstrated the proud defiant character of the city when Mancunians turned out in droves to welcome back the plucky Ariane Grande who went back to do a repeat concert.

I no longer live in Manchester, having moved away for career demands but I consider myself fortunate to have spent my formative years there. These are my personal memories and I know they will not coincide exactly with those of others but I hope, for older readers, to have evoked a little nostalgia and, for younger ones, to have given them a taste of everyday life before they were born.

Printed in Great Britain
by Amazon